The Seven-day Rhythms of Life

Examining Their Purpose and the Supporting Evidence

Dr. G. Kenneth Greenaway

World rights reserved. This book or any portion thereof may not be copied or reproduced in any form or manner whatever, except as provided by law, without the written permission of the publisher, except by a reviewer who may quote brief passages in a review.

The author assumes full responsibility for the accuracy of all facts and quotations as cited in this book. The opinions expressed in this book are the author's personal views and interpretations, and do not necessarily reflect those of the publisher.

This book is provided with the understanding that the publisher is not engaged in giving spiritual, legal, medical, or other professional advice. If authoritative advice is needed, the reader should seek the counsel of a competent professional.

Copyright © 2022 Dr. G. Kenneth Greenaway

Copyright © 2022 TEACH Services, Inc.

ISBN-13: 978-1-4796-1355-7 (Paperback)

ISBN-13: 978-1-4796-1356-4 (ePub)

Library of Congress Control Number: 2021919394

All scripture quotations, unless otherwise indicated, are taken from the King James Version of the Bible. Public domain.

Table of Contents

Introduction 5

Where did the Weekly Cycle Originate? 7

Circadian Rhythm 11

Larger Biological Rhythms 13

Microscopic Life 16

Plants, Insects, Fish, and Birds 17

A Famous Horse 22

Human Beings 23

Environmental or Built-in? 35

Adaptations of the Week 41

Identifying the Purposes of the Marker in Nature 45

Embracing the Rhythm of Rest 50

The Purpose of Humanity's Design 51

End Notes 53

Introduction

We take the marking of time by the seven days of the *week* for granted. But the week is not our only measure of time. We also mark time by the light and dark of the day, by the phases of the moon that roughly make a *month*, and by the four cyclic *seasons* of the *year*, determined by the tilt of the earth as it completes a full revolution around the sun. Yet, where does the week come from? Most people know that the seven-day week is in the creation story of Genesis, but is there some marker in nature that corresponds to the weekly cycle?[1] Exploring that possibility and identifying the purposes for such a marker is the motivation for this modest book.

Where did the Weekly Cycle Originate?

Though biblical records indicate an earlier weekly cycle, one of the earliest written records of using names for the days of the week has been found in the ruins of the ash-covered ancient city of Pompeii, which was destroyed by the eruption of Mount Vesuvius in A. D. 79. However, there is an even earlier fragment of a seven-day calendar that has been dated between 19 B.C. and A. D. 4, and there is a verse written in 19 B.C. by the poet Tibullus, which contains a specific reference to "the day of Saturn."

The sequence of days was attached to the seven known celestial bodies: (1) Saturn, (2) the Sun, (3) the moon, (4) Mars, (5) Mercury, (6) Jupiter, and (7) Venus. Notice that, originally, the cycle began with "Saturn's day." Before the end of the first century A.D., the cycle shifted forward one day when early non-Jewish Christians identified Saturn's day with the seventh-day Sabbath, shifting the beginning of the week to Sunday from then forward.[2] The order of the cycle did not change, just where to start the cycle.[3]

Some have asserted that the weekly cycle is a purely human idea, that it comes from an inexact division of the month into four equal parts of seven days (though this would only work if each month were just 28 days long).[4] This notion is based on the presuppositions of scholars who do not believe in the veracity of the biblical account of the Creation in Genesis or the history of the Jewish people in the Old Testament. They assume that the seven-day week came from Babylon's lunar "week," which started over every new month, rather than coming from the biblical Creation account. These scholars consider the Genesis account to be a later fictional fabrication that only purports to tell how life on earth began, even though the stories of Genesis are not written like pagan legends but as real accounts based on real events with real geographical settings and even though new discoveries confirm the biblical record more and more by the year. As Zerubavel has noted, only one ethnic group is responsible for the promulgation of the seven-day week in the Roman world: "The establishment of a seven-day week based on the regular observance of the Sabbath is a distinctively Jewish contribution to civilization."[5] Yet, Zerubavel sees the week as a human devising. "The invention of the continuous week was therefore one of the most significant breakthroughs in human beings' attempts to break away from being prisoners of nature and create a social world of their own."[6] Like many scholars, he works from the assumption that the biblical Creation account is not the origin of the weekly cycle. In this booklet, it is not our purpose to review the biblical data for the seven-day cycle but to investigate whether there is biological support for it that is engrained in the natural world and in human biology. As we review the discoveries of research, you may be surprised.

Circadian Rhythm

Research into the sphere of time rhythms within the human body began over half a century ago, with the work of Dr. Franz Halberg, at a time that discussion about circadian rhythms was in its infancy. Circadian rhythm is now fully accepted as a descriptor of physiological functions that fluctuate over the course of a 24-hour day.

Circadian rhythm affects the functioning of the human body as well as the functioning of all other organisms.

Many studies have shown that the periods of light and darkness affect different functions of the human body as well as providing times of superior productivity and physical action. Knowledge of the circadian rhythm has been helpful for those who wish to lose weight, knowing that their whole system consumes calories better in the earlier part of the day. It has made people aware of the greater likelihood of accidents during the hours of the night. It has helped physicians to prepare courses of treatment that are more helpful to their patients. Circadian rhythm affects the functioning of the human body as well as the functioning of all other organisms. Studies regarding the cycles of light and darkness have demonstrated that humans are adaptable to the manipulation of the visual cues of light and dark. When kept in a totally isolated environment, human perception of the day can be less than 24 hours, a feature that enables the body to adapt to seasonal changes, showing that there is a connection between the functions within the human body and the physical environment.

Larger Biological Rhythms

With the discoveries regarding circadian rhythms in organisms and in the human body, Dr. Halberg began exploring larger periods of time and what other rhythms he might find. He began to recognize that there was also a seven-day cycle for many biological functions. Prior to the use of antibiotic drugs, physicians had regularly observed that, if someone were sick, the seven-day period after their sickness began was a breakpoint as to whether they would get better or not. With the advent of life-saving antibiotics, that observation regarding the seven-day make-it-or-break-it period was obscured. And yet, Dr. Halberg was aware of that seven-day period and began to keep records of different functions of human physiology to determine if there were some bases for seven-day cycles. He began to see correlations, not only for humans but for many other living organisms. With an evolutionary perspective, he inferred that this rhythmic oscillation in chemical balance and bodily function had given early life some kind of advantage. As it had to do with human beings, the question was whether the seven-day cycle were a built-in part of human biology or something that was learned, an adaptation from environmental cues. In other words, was it nature, or was it nurture?

Even organisms that were not subject to regular periods of light and dark, which would define a natural day, were able to maintain production of certain enzymes that showed that their bodies were able to discern the seven-day week.

The answers came very slowly, for studies to back up the seven-day cycles would require years of careful observation, measuring, note keeping, graphing, and interpretation. Some of the observations would have been too tedious to maintain for weeks on end because it would require taking temperatures and drawing blood at regular intervals for extended periods of time. Yet, there were dedicated individuals who kept their own diaries and contributed to these studies, and there were babies in neo-natal wards of hospitals that required round-the-clock testing. This proved helpful in several ways. The results over these many years of study began to show that even organisms that were not subject to regular periods of light and dark, which would define a natural day, were able to maintain production of certain enzymes that showed that their bodies were able to discern the seven-day week. The seven-day week has been connected to numerous bodily functions for humans—including those of the heart, the kidneys, the immune system, and wound healing. These seven-day cycles were originally referred to as Circaseptan Rhythms.

ACETABULARIA

Many species of living organisms are known to express a seven-day cycle, beginning with two marine organisms—the unicellular green alga *Acetabularia*[7] and the simple unicellular *Gonyaulax polyedra*.[8] Acetabularia displays a seven-day rhythm in growth rates[9] and the glowing luminescence of the dinoflagellate alga *Gonyaulax polyedra* also seems to follow a weekly rhythm.[10]

Plants, Insects, Fish, and Birds

Researchers have also found that **pole bean** seeds (*Phaseolus vulgaris*) draw up water in a seven-day cyclic fashion, leading up to the full moon. They have also found the hemolymph constituents in **worker honey bees**, which function something like the circulatory systems in animals with a heart and blood vessels, follow cycles of around seven days under natural conditions.[11] Another example of a seven-day pattern was discovered in the **pike fish** (*Esox lucius L.*). With only darkness and no light, the pineal gland of the fish produced melatonin, a hormone that controls the sleep-wake cycle, in very regular cycles of about seven days.[12]

The **springtail** (*Folsomia candida*) also has seven-day cycles. Under constant darkness, its egg-laying, its period of time for skin molting, and its growth all follow seven-day cycles. Also, when stressed by changes in the temperature of its environment, the springtail lives longest when the changes are made at a seven-day interval.[13] The activity level of the **beach beetle** (*Chaerodes trachyscelides White*) also followed seven-day cycles.[14] The **face fly** (*Musca autumnalis De Geer*) and the green alga *Acetabularia mediterranea*[15] live longer when the artificial 24-hour light and day cycle approximates seven days.[16]

The amounts of growth in marine bivalves, among other variables that are dependent on water flow, light, and temperature[17] also seem to follow rhythmic cycles of seven to nine days.[18]

Laboratory Rodents

Researchers have found instances of seven-day rhythms in **lab mice** studied within a laboratory environment that provided normal 24-hour light and dark cycles. The rhythms include cyclic levels of pineal melatonin, a hormone that helps to regulate circadian rhythms;[19] corneal mitosis, which is the gradual replacement of the cells of the cornea in the eye;[20]

cardiac creatine phosphokinase enzyme activity, an indicator of heart damage;[21] tolerance to irradiation of the whole body to X-rays;[22] excretion of sodium in the urine when fed a diet high in salt;[23] function of the immune system, which fights foreign microscopic invaders;[24] death from malaria germs injected into the test animals;[25]

acceptance or rejection of a transplanted kidney,[26] heart tissue or pancreas tissue,[27] or skin-to-muscle grafting.[28] The rhythms also include the therapeutic effect of medications;[29] the time it took for blood antibodies to respond to vaccine-delivered antigens, which are substances that can stimulate an immune response;[30] and the concentration of the lab animal's blood plasma, which is the liquid component of blood that holds the blood cells in suspension, and brain pregnenolone, which protects brain cells from long-term damage, in lab animals that have had their adrenal glands or testicles surgically removed.[31]

Scientists have noted seven-day cycles of sodium and potassium excretion in rats on a high-salt diet.[32] They have also found in studies of rats without seven-day medical care that the rejection of kidneys, pancreas, and hearts are associated with seven-day cycles. Such studies have implications for the application of medications for humans.

A Famous Horse

Scientists have also detected a seven-day cycle in an intensive study of a famous Brazilian-bred **Mangalarga stallion**.[33]

They found statistically significant fluctuations of seven-day cycles in semen volume, sperm motility, and spermatozoa concentration. However, in other studies, investigators were only able to find weak and inconsistent seven-day biochemical and physiologic rhythms in a study of exercise training of horses.[34]

Human Beings

There is evidence of built-in seven-day rhythms for many functions of the human body. The list keeps growing. Below are functions for which scientists have discovered a seven-day cycle.

- Some free-running seven-day rhythms have to do with wound healing.[35]
- Others have to do with positive and negative moods.[36]
- Seven-day cycles have been noted in physical activity levels.[37]
- These cycles have been demonstrated in nighttime sleep duration.[38]
- Various studies show a seven-day cyclic nature for blood pressure.
- Other studies show a seven-day cycle for the acid content in the blood.
- There is also a seven-day cyclic pattern of red blood cell production.
- Oral and core body temperature have been shown to conform to a seven-day cycle.[39]
- Seven-day rhythms have been noted in urine chemistry and urinary volume.[40]

- One study suggested a seven-day rhythm for sexual activity.
- Another study showed a seven-day pattern for the ratio between norepinephrine and epinephrine, which are two important neurotransmitters.
- DNA labeling and cell mitosis, the division that creates two new nuclei, have also been correlated to a seven-day cycle.[41]
- Menstruation and the entire female reproductive cycle has been shown to follow a seven-day rhythm.
- There is a seven-day cycle for babies delivered at full term.
- In one Australian study, between 151 and 247 of 1,118 patients with seizures showed strong seven-day rhythms.[42]
- Seven-day cycles have been correlated to total calories and dietary constituent consumption.[43]

- These cycles have been observed in stress-associated evening/nighttime eating.[44]
- The same rhythms have been correlated to the functioning of the immune system (which fights foreign bodies) and hemostatic systems (which check bleeding).[45]

Let's consider some of these in greater detail.

Healing. Tracking the gradual decrease in swelling after maxillo-facial surgery revealed crests in sleep-time heart rate, basal metabolic rate (the total number of calories that your body needs to perform basic life-sustaining functions), locomotor activity (how a person moves from one place to another), physical work capacity, grip strength, left ventricular function (the efficiency of the part of the heart that pumps oxygenated blood through the aorta to the body), and reaction time on days 7, 14 and 21 of healing.[46] In a study regarding healing using rehabilitative and spa therapies, the peak in healing occurred one week after treatment began. Also reticulocyte count (the number of immature red blood cells without a nucleus) peaked after high altitude exposure after seven days.[47] Fitness and strength during and after physical and muscle strength training also peaked after seven days.[48]

Transplanted organs. A patient's rejection of a kidney from either a dead or live donor, which is tracked by a build up of plasma creatinine, a waste product from normal wear and tear on muscles of the body, also exhibits prominent seven-day rhythms, with rejection aligning frequently in 6-8 days (or a multiple thereof) after the kidney was implanted. In four studies with a total of 628 patients, 280 transplant recipients rejected the transplant, and the rejection period for 6–8 days after surgery (or a multiple thereof) was nearly 50% higher than rejection within 2–5-days post surgery (or multiples thereof).[49] The same seven-day pattern was discerned following DNA synthesis of tubular epidermal cells on a kidney following the removal of a tumor.[50]

> *Studies showed seven-day rhythms in heart rate, in diastolic and systolic blood pressure, and in day-night systolic blood pressure ratio.*

Blood pressure. Studies showed seven-day rhythms in heart rate, in diastolic and systolic blood pressure, and in day-night systolic blood pressure ratio.[51] Interestingly, when the seven-day cyclic rhythm of the systolic blood pressure and diastolic blood pressure is not stable, it is a strong indication that the patient will not survive. One study showed seven-day rhythms of systolic blood pressure and diastolic blood pressure rhythms in comatose patients in an intensive care unit, showing that the cycles were not influenced by conscious thought. The seven-day rhythms were three times more pronounced than were the same patients' 24-hour rhythms.[52] Another study showed regular seven-day fluctuations of diastolic and systolic blood pressure in response to putting a person's hand in ice water for about a minute, which would indicate independence from external stimuli.[53]

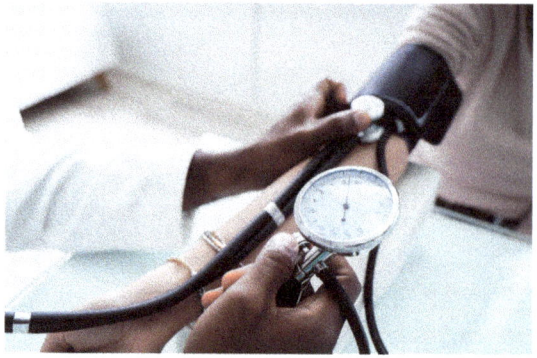

Blood values. Scientists have noted that platelets, which carry oxygen in the blood, showed weekly rhythmic cycles in their levels of glutathione. Glutathione is a coenzyme antioxidant substance made from amino acids that helps maintain the health of the cells by reducing cancer-causing free radicals in the body.[54] The correlation was so strong that testing for this seven-day cycle has been designated "an important prognostic factor in oncology," which means that it can help doctors project whether a person is going to get cancer.[55]

Glutathione $C_{10}H_{17}N_3O_6S$

Urine chemistry. Levi and Halberg describe the production of a built-in seven-day cycle, separate from human cues, in the excretion of 17-ketosteroids, which are substances that form when the body breaks down male steroid sex hormones and other hormones released by the adrenal glands.[56] In a study of men under long-term flight simulation, urinary sodium excretion occurred out of sync with the seven-day biological rhythm in plasma aldosterone, a corticosteroid hormone which stimulates absorption of sodium by the kidneys, thereby regulating water and salt balance, but in sync with the concentration of plasma cortisol, a hormone that is increased in response to stress and low blood-glucose concentration.[57] Seven-day cycles have been correlated in thoracic impedance in certain heart failure patients.[58] Thoracic impedance is "a measure of the electrical activity in the chest that varies with changes in body size and composition, fluid volume, ventilatory status, and other variables."[59] Also, about seven-day free-running rhythms were detected in urinary cortisol concentration in arthritic patients after treatment with

ACTH (adrenocorticotropic hormone), a hormone made by the pituitary gland.[60] Cortisol is a hormone that stimulates the liver to convert fat into glucose for energy, and it aids in regulating blood pressure and in storing memories.[61]

Danish endocrinologist Christian Hamburger conducted a long-term self study on his own seven-day cycles. From age 43 to 58, he collected his 24-hour urine output to measure his total amount of urine as well as his 17-ketosteroid concentration (an index of androgen production). Talk about discipline and devotion! Throughout the study, he kept a very regular 24-hour and weekly routine, resting one-half day Saturdays and all-day Sundays. The pattern produced when charted revealed not only statistically significant annual but seven-day rhythms in urine volume and 17-ketosteroid, with the peak of the 17-ketosteroid rhythm around midday Sunday and the peak of the seven-day urine volume rhythm around midnight Wednesday, the average between the two seven-day rhythms thus being about 3½ days.[62] Of further interest is the finding that both 17-ketosteroid and urine volume exhibited a cycle of precisely seven days during the initial 12 years of the self-study. However, the 17-ketosteroid cycle changed during the last three years of the period, as Christian Hamburger began consistently self-medicating with a specific dose of testosterone at regular intervals. During this period, the 17-ketosteroid rhythm shortened to less than seven days, which showed its independence from the social cues of the weekly cycle. Yet, the seven-day rhythm of his urine output remained the same with the cycle being exactly seven days in length.[63]

Sexual activity. A detailed review of Christian Hamburger's daily diary during the 15-year self-study also revealed seven-day (and 3½ day) patterning of his sexual activity. Sexual activity was highest on Sundays, thus coinciding with the peak of his seven-day rhythm of 17-ketosteroid, with a second smaller peak in sexual activity on Thursdays, associated as well with a second smaller peak in 17-ketosteroid.[64]

Pregnant and Lactating Mothers. Biological cycles of about one week have also been demonstrated in systolic and diastolic blood pressure during pregnancy.[65] Likewise, seven-day cycles have been demonstrated regarding the ability of human breast milk of lactating mothers to bind corticosteroids, a class of steroid hormones that are produced in the adrenal cortex to respond to stress, react against foreign microscopic invaders, to regulate inflammation, metabolize carbohydrates, break down protein, maintain blood electrolyte levels, and moderate behavior.[66]

Infants. That many newborns require around-the-clock care in hospitals provided the opportunity for blood collection and physical examination, including measuring the blood pressure, heart rate, and body weight gain of babies, including twins, from birth onward. These measurements revealed numerous seven-day rhythms.[67]

Children. Studies of children revealed other seven-day patterns in nutrient and calorie consumption of four-year-old infants as well as tooth development, particularly enamel deposition (striae of Retzius).[68] Moreover, seven-day rhythms of cognitive functions are reported in school-aged children and adolescents of both genders and also adult men and women.[69]

Medical Emergencies. Other instances of seven-day cycles have been noted in relatively rare, isolated cases of medical conditions that have gotten worse[70] as well as in cases in the general population for infectious illnesses, lower digestive tract disease, lung problems, mood diseases (including suicidal intent), blood flow, and neurological disorders.[71] Other instances have been noted in life-threatening cardiac and vascular events. Also, there is generally a spike on Mondays in hospital admissions for acute care of a high blood pressure crises, severe heart chest pains, cardiac arrhythmias, worsening heart failure, acute aortic rupture or dissection, Takotsubo cardiomyopathy, myocardial infarction, sudden cardiac arrest, transient ischemic attack, and stroke.[72]

Environmental or Built-in?

The perennial question is: Are seven-day rhythms built-in or are they environmentally induced? Evidence on the side of their being built-in is that animals kept under laboratory conditions without regular seven-day observer interaction have still had the seven-day cycles, and so have animals that were injected with poisonous stimuli or antigens. Also evidence on the side of their being built-in is that humans

> *The perennial question is: Are seven-day rhythms built-in or are they environmentally induced?*

have exhibited seven-day rhythms that are not synchronized to the environmental time cues of the calendar week.[73] Evidence on the side of their being internal came in a study of patients in persistent vegetative-state in which the patients' heart rate, and systolic and diastolic blood pressures correlated to seven-day cycles.[74] Further evidence for their being built-in comes from a study of the shortening or lengthening of the 24-hour cycle and of the seven-day and 30-day cycles for human beings living in an artificial environment without the cues of natural light and dark. Under these conditions, the cycles tend to lengthen for the 24-hour cycle but shorten for the seven-day and 30-day cycles. These findings imply that these cycles, though controlled by their own biological "clocks," are related to each other but affected differently by environmental cues which, under natural conditions, would tend to synchronize them.[75] So, among all the other rhythms, the seven-day rhythm appears to be the rhythm by which all others are tuned or orchestrated.[76] Such observations lean toward the conclusion that the seven-day week, found in many ancient and modern civilizations including the three main monotheistic religions, may be an adaptation to a built-in biologic rhythm rather than the rhythm being a societally impressed phenomenon.[77]

Free-running oscillations of about seven days in oral and axillary temperature, heart rate, systolic blood pressure, diastolic blood pressure, average arterial blood pressure, and urinary norepinephrine concentration have been observed with subjects who have isolated from known environmental, social, and clock-time cues.[78] These findings are consistent with the hypothesis that human seven-day rhythms are innate and biological in origin. It does seem, however, that these built-in rhythms can respond to external influences such as circadian influences of day and night or the lunar-induced tides.[79] Several publications have reported that seven-day rhythms in humans and laboratory animals can be triggered or enhanced by external factors.[80] Yet, no one has identified exactly what mechanisms trigger these seven-day rhythmic biological cycles.[81] One researcher postulated that the trigger—whatever it is—may be simply amplifying a rhythm that would otherwise be too subtle for detection.[82]

Weekly Health Behaviors. Additionally, injuries of boys and girls between the ages of 5 to 16 have significant seven-day and 3½-day patterns with a midday Wednesday peak.[83] There are also day-of-week differences in searches for health information on the internet.[84] Searches in the Norwegian language over a 911-day period for medical information about chlamydia, gonorrhea, herpes, HIV, and AIDS, as well as the flu, diabetes, and menopause follow a seven-day pattern, with the most searches on Monday and Tuesday.[85] Seven-day patterns can also be discerned in Google searches that include the word "healthy." In a review of searches between 2005 and 2012, there were significantly more searches on Mondays and Tuesdays than on the other days of the week.[86] Google searches for those wanting to quit smoking also revealed a strong day-of-week pattern, with Monday queries in English, French, Mandarin or Cantonese, Portuguese, Russian, and Spanish that were 25% greater than all the searches from Tuesday through Sunday combined.[87] Of course, as one might assume, these particular seven-day cycles can be influenced by the risky behaviors that people have engaged in over the weekend or they may be due to the different way that computers are used during the weekdays versus the weekend.[88] Nonetheless, some researchers believe these cycles reflect some kind of internal time structure.[89]

Adaptations of the Week

These functions are further enhanced by regular external schedules. Over the course of history, various experiments in altering the week to different periods have been attempted. Rome, for example, used an eight-day week. However, Rome eventually gravitated toward the Hebrew seven-day week.

In the last two hundred and fifty years, there have been two notable experiments regarding weeks that didn't have seven days. During the French Reign of Terror,

French leadership decided that they would make a week they believed more rational than the biblical seven-day week. They decided to create a rhythmic system of time based on a ten-day "décade." This was an affront to those who marked the rhythm of life through the seven-day week, with a day of worship every week. It took a while to institute this change, and, with the social upheaval of the French Revolution, the ten-day "décade" only lasted a little more than, well, a decade—from October 10, 1793 until September 9, 1805, when Napoleon signed an accord with the Roman Catholic Church to bring about stability in the nation by restoring the seven-day "beat" of life. As author Eviatar Zarubavel observed in his book, *The Seven-day Cycle*, it is the seven-day week that brings stability to human society.[90]

There was a second experiment in a non-seven-day week, which demonstrates society's need of the week. Under Joseph Stalin, Russia, like France, sought to distinguish itself from the seven-day week of Jews, Christians, and Muslims. This was largely because the major goal of the Russian leaders was industrial production. Consequently, they put the whole country into shift work. To keep the factories running, all able-bodied men and women were put on three different five-day shifts. It was awkward trying to keep up with the schedules, and people in the same families did not even have the same day off. To disassociate this system from the seven-day week, the days were given names that were unattached to the traditional weekday names. These names did not stick, and the government ultimately ended up just numbering the days and color-coding the workers' days off, causing people to form friendships among those whose schedules coincided with their own. Thus, religious days of worship were disregarded, and families were separated. Problems in productivity also arose because people with the same jobs overlapped one another, and there was always a day of catching up for the new shift of workers regarding where projects stood. With multiple people in charge of the same equipment, workers lost their sense of responsibility for the upkeep of the equipment they were using. Ultimately, the scheduling of three overlapping shifts for the whole country to improve productivity ended up costing industry. The five-day overlapping labor system was eventually abandoned, with the return to the seven-day cycle credited to the influence of the agricultural class in rural areas who had been able to maintain a seven-day week because they had not been tied to industry.

We could look at the historical evidence and still not conclude that the people were uncomfortable with the 10-day week because it was different from what they were used to and, therefore, resisted it. It took the experiments of Halberg and his associates to recognize the systemic functions that run on seven-day cycles. These are all interesting discoveries, and they leave us questioning what our response should be. Quite obviously, the functions within our bodies, which work so automatically that we are unaware of them, are not generally under our conscious control. However, there is one major thing that we can do. As human beings, we can recognize that our own endeavors work best with cyclic periods of work and rest. Ten days is too long. Three days is too short. A period of seven days fits our bodily rhythms and enables us to function productively in a stressful world while maintaining physical and mental balance.

Identifying the Purposes of the Marker in Nature

As we note all the findings of seven-day cycles (previously called circaseptan rhythms), it prompts us to ask, "What is the marker in nature that correlates with the weekly cycle?" This leads us to the pineal gland, a very tiny gland in the middle of the brain about the size of two fused rice grains. It has been found that this gland acts as a rhythmic control center which influences several different endocrine and immune system functions. How can something so tiny govern so many bodily functions? It does so via various stimuli—chemical, neuronal, photonic, and geomagnetic.[91][92][93] This reminds us of the biblical text, 1 Corinthians 1:27 (KJV), which states that God has chosen the weak things of the world to confound the things which are mighty. The amazing secrets of the pineal gland, revealed within the last century, lead us to ask, "Could this all have happened by chance?" If it didn't, we ought to recognize that there is a Creator.

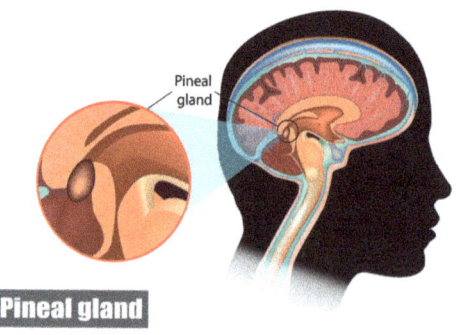

Pineal gland

Taking all the previously stated facts into consideration, the following questions/points are raised:

- Is it not reasonable to assume that there is a "Higher Power" who has created these inbuilt mechanisms rather than being randomly selected as suggested by the theory of evolution?

- Who was this Creator and does He still maintain His creation?

- The existence of a Creator is evidenced by the intricate inter-connectivity of all aspects of nature, all synchronized into one harmonious whole which we call LIFE.

- How did that life originate and which school of thought is correct—creation or evolution? One is genuine and the other is counterfeit. The facts suggest that creation is the genuine explanation of the origin of life and there is a central thread present in created entities (for example, seven-day rhythms).

- These seven-day rhythms remind us of the *seven-ness* found throughout the Bible, so could it be that the God of the Bible, also known as Jesus Christ, is the Creator who made earth, sea, and sky?
- Interestingly, there is a similar language used (maker of heaven, earth, and seas) in three main signposts of the Bible which identify God as Creator:
  - Genesis 2:1–3 (KJV)—Creator of all things including the seventh day sabbath of rest (Saturday).
  - Exodus 20:8–11 (KJV)—God shows that the seventh-day Sabbath is a SIGN or SEAL of His authority. He is God (His name) and He is Creator (His title) of heaven and earth, the

sea, and all that is in them (His territory.)

- Revelation 14:6–12 (KJV)—In the three angels' messages, God is identified as Creator of earth, sea, and sky and the critical issue of worship is raised.

- The second angel's message of Revelation 14:8 was muted but repeated more forcefully in Revelation 18:1–5 (KJV) by a "Fourth Angel" because of the further deterioration of the condition of the world. This is therefore God's URGENT and FINAL message to the whole world. God is pleading with us, "Come out of her my people, out of the system of false worship." In the final analysis, true worship is that which is due only to the Creator of the world. Worship of any other entity is false.

Embracing the Rhythm of Rest

Many people who have no religious leanings recognize that they need a restful change in their activities on a weekly basis. Christians, by and large, look at Sunday as a day for their rest and, in many Christian traditions, take Sunday as a kind of sabbath. Other Christians, who recognize the historical basis for the story of Creation, the story of Abraham, the Exodus and later history of the Jewish people, the life of Christ, and the acts of the apostles, have noticed that the day of rest for believers in the biblical God in Bible times, as mentioned repeatedly, is the seventh-day Sabbath, which, in our current cycle, is Saturday. In Hebrew, it is the only day of the week that has a specific name. It is *Shabbat*, which means "ceasing" or "rest." In the Greek language, which is the language of the New Testament, even to this day the seventh day is called *sabbaton*, or "sabbath," and the day preceding it is *paraskeuēn*, or "preparation." Taking all of these discoveries into account, we could conclude that Jesus' statement to the leaders of His day holds true for us as well. He said to them: "The Sabbath was made for man." It is altogether clear from our human experience—both historically and personally—that we need rhythmic weekly rest.

The Purpose of Humanity's Design

When we reflect on the above-mentioned discoveries of seven-day rhythms such as the cyclical healing of wounds in humans and animals, we can conclude and accept, without a doubt, that there is a Creator whom we acknowledge as God, the Ruler of the Universe. This is opposed to the evolutionist's idea of randomness in the origin of life. We can further conclude that this Creator God has designed His creation in an orderly cyclical fashion having six days of labor followed by one day of rest (a day refers to the 24-hour period of a circadian rhythm).

This God of Creation, as described in the books of Genesis and Exodus and referenced throughout the remainder of the Bible, deserves our worship, our reverence, and our obedience. We demonstrate our obedience by keeping the seventh day (Saturday) holy and by ceasing from labor as we are reminded to do in the fourth commandment of Exodus 20:8–11 in the King James Version of the Bible (KJV). This seventh-day (Saturday) rest also gives us an opportunity to develop a more intimate relationship with the Creator by reflecting on His love, His grace, and His mercy. Additionally, we recognize 1) Where we came from, 2) What our values ought to be, and 3) How we were made to function in order to achieve the Purpose for which we were designed. This purpose is to worship the Creator God who is the only One who deserves to be worshipped.[94]

End Notes

[1] See Genesis chapters 1 and 2 and Genesis 29:27, 28.

[2] Because of the Jewish influence, the Romans described Saturday as a *dias nefastus*—a day that shouldn't be worked on. See F. H. Colson, *The Week: An Essay on the Origin & Development of the Seven-Day Cycle*, p. 14: "There were Romans, who felt no real attraction to Judaism, but still had some superstitious regard for the Sabbath." See also A. H. Sayce, *The "Higher Criticism" and the Verdict of the Monuments*, 1895, p. 74; Martial; Josephus, *Against Apion*, bk. 2, 40, "There is not any city of the Grecians, nor any of the barbarians, nor any nation whatsoever, whither our custom of resting on the seventh day hath not come … "; Philo, "On the Creation," 30:89, "For that day is the festival, not of one city or one country, but of all the earth; a day which alone it is right to call the day of festival for all people, and the birthday of the world"; Ovid, who three times couples the Sabbath with other days of leisure or inactivity; Horace, "the superstition of the Sabbath was widespread among less enlightened people"; Tibullus, *Carmina* 1, 3, 15-18, "The sacred day of Saturn held one back"; Aristobulus quotes Homer and Hesiod, who speak of the seventh day as sacred and venerable; Tibullus; Sextus Propertius, *Elegies*, 4, 1, 81-86, "The sign of Saturn that brings woe to one and to all"; Seneca in Augustine's *City of God*, bk. 6, chap. 11, "The customs of this accursed nation [the Jews] have gained such influence that they are now received throughout the world.

The vanquished have given laws to their victors … the greater part of the people go through a ritual not knowing why they do so."

[3] See, for example, Justin Martyr, "First Apology," 67.

[4] "Those who believe that our seven-day week has derived from the lunar cycle seem to forget that the latter is not really a twenty-eight day cycle" (Zerubavel, p. 9).

[5] Zerubavel, p. 8.

[6] Zerubavel, p. 11.

[7] D. H. Berger, K. Pribram, H. Wild, C. Bridges (1990), "An analysis of neural spike-train distributions: determinants of the response of visual cortex neurons to changes in orientation and spatial frequency," *Experimental Brain Research*, vol. 80(1), pp. 129–134. https://1ref.us/1p7 (accessed June 14, 2021); Hans-Georg Schweiger (1969), "Cell biology of acetabularia," *Current Topics in Microbiology and Immunology*, vol. 50, pp. 1–36; Hans-Georg Schweiger, E. Schweiger (1965), "The role of the nucleus in a cytoplasmic diurnal rhythm," in Jürgen Aschoff, ed., *Circadian Clocks*, Amsterdam: North Holland Publishing Co., pp. 195–197; Hans-Georg Schweiger, Sigrid Berger, Horst Kretschmer, Hannelore Mörler, Erna Halberg, Robert B. Sothern, and Franz Halberg (1986), "Evidence for a circaseptan and a circasemiseptan growth response to light/dark cycle shifts in nucleated and enucleated Acetabularia cells, respectively," *Proceedings of the National Academy of Sciences of the United States of America*, vol. 83, pp. 8619–8623.

[8] Germaine Cornélissen, Hellmuth Broda, Franz Halberg (1986), "Does *Gonyaulax polyedra* measure a week?" *Cell Biophysics*, vol. 8, pp. 69–85; Franz Halberg, John Woodland Hastings, Germaine Cornélissen, Hellmuth

Broda (1985), "Gonyaulax polyedra 'talks' both 'circadian' and 'circaseptan,'" *Chronobiologia*, vol. 12, p. 185; John Woodland Hastings, Alexander Keynan (1965) "Molecular aspects of circadian rhythms," in *Circadian Clocks*, pp. 165–182.

[9] Hans-Georg Schweiger, Sigrid Berger, Horst Kretschmer, Hannelore Mörler, Erna Halberg, Robert B. Sothern, and Franz Halberg (1986), "Evidence for a circaseptan and a circasemiseptan growth response to light/dark cycle shifts in nucleated and enucleated Acetabularia cells," *Proceedings of the National Academy of Sciences of the United States of America*, vol. 83, pp. 8619–8623.

[10] Germaine Cornélissen, Hellmuth Broda, Franz Halberg (1986), "Does Gonyaulax polyedra measure a week?" *Cell Biophysiology*, vol. 8, pp. 69–85.

[11] Miroslav Mikulecky, Michel Bounias (1997), "Worker honeybee hemolymph lipid composition and synodic lunar cycle periodicities," *Brazilian Journal of Medical and Biological Research*, vol. 30, pp. 275–279.

[12] Germaine Cornélissen, Ana Portela, Franz Halberg, Valerie Bolliet, Jack Falcon (1995a), "Toward a chronome of superfused pike pineals: About-weekly (circaseptan) modulation of circadian melatonin release," *In vivo*, vol. 9, pp. 323–329.

[13] Mirian David Marques, Laurence K. Cutkomp, Germaine Cornélissen, et al. (1987), "Lifespan of springtail on 12-hr shifts at varying intervals of 12-hr alternation in ambient temperature," *Progress in Clinical and Biological Research*, vol. 227A, pp. 257–264.

[14] Yoshihiko Chiba, Laurence K. Cutkomp, Franz Halberg (1973), "Circaseptan (7-day) oviposition rhythm and growth in Springtail, *Folsomia candida (Collembola: Isotomidae)*,"

Journal of Interdisciplinary Cycle Research, vol. 4, pp. 59–66; Mirian David Marques, Laurence K. Cutkomp, et al. (1987); Meyer-Rochow & Brown, 1998)

[15] Hans-Georg Schweiger, Sigrid Berger, Horst Kretschmer, Hannelore Mörler, Erna Halberg, Robert B. Sothern, and Franz Halberg (1986), "Evidence for a circaseptan and a circasemiseptan growth response to light/dark cycle shifts in nucleated and enucleated Acetabularia cells," *Proceedings of the National Academy of Sciences of the United States of America*, vol. 83, pp. 8619–8623.

[16] Dora K. Hayes, Franz Halberg, Terrence Teslow (1980), "Replicated frequency of lighting regimen shifts and aging in the face fly reveals circadian-circaseptan interaction" (Abstract 768), *Physiologist*, vol. 23, p. 146; Dora K. Hayes, Germaine Cornélissen, Franz Halberg, Kalva Shankaraiah (1983), "Survival time of the face fly model as a gauge of circaseptan organization and optimization," *Chronobiologia*, vol. 10, pp. 132–133; Dora K. Hayes, Franz Halberg, Germaine Cornélissen, Kalva Shankaraiah (1986), "Frequency response of the face fly, *Musca autumnalis*, to lighting-schedule shifts at varied intervals," *Annals of the Entomological Society of America*, vol. 79, pp. 317–323.

[17] George R. Clark, II (1975), "Periodic growth and biological rhythms in experimentally grown bivalves," in Gary D. Rosenberg and Stanley Keith Runcorn, eds., *Growth Rhythms and the History of the Earth's Rotation*, London: Plenum, pp. 103–134; Ida Thompson (1975), "Biological clocks and shell growth in bivalves," in *Growth Rhythms and the History of the Earth's Rotation*, pp. 149–161.

[18] Giorgio Pannella (1977), "Periodical growth patterns in some calcified tissues," *Proceedings of the XII International Society for Chronobiology*, Washington, DC, pp. 649–655.

[19] Salvador Sánchez de la Peña, Gregory Micheal Brown, Frank Ungar, et al. (1986), "Chronobiologic lead study cost-effectively assesses circadian-circaseptan intermodulation in murine pineal melatonin content," *Chronobiologia*, vol. 13, pp. 329–333.

[20] Tong-Hua Tsai, Lawrence E. Scheving, Salvador Sánchez de la Peña, et al. (1989), "Circaseptan (about 7-day) modulation of circadian rhythm in corneal mitoses of Holtzman rats," *The Anatomical Record*, vol. 225, pp. 181–188.

[21] Nelson Marques, Salvador Sánchez de la Peña, T. Mushiya, W. G. Yasmineh, G. Cornelissen, Franz Halberg (1994), "Ultradian-infradian variation of cardiac creatine phosphokinase (CPK) activity in male Holtzman rats," *Chronobiologia*, vol. 21, pp. 241–250.

[22] Lawrence E. Scheving, Franz Halberg, John E. Pauly, et al. (1981), "Circadian and about-weekly (circaseptan) interactions characterize murine tolerance to whole-body x-irradiation (abstract)," *Proceedings of the American Association for Cancer Research and the American Society of Clinical Oncology*, vol. 22, p. 63.

[23] Keiko Uezono, Linda L. Sackett-Lundee, Terukazu Kawasaki, Teruo Omae, Erhard Haus (1987), "Circaseptan rhythm in sodium and potassium excretion in salt-sensitive and salt-resistant Dahl rats," *Progress in clinical and biological research*, vol. 227A, pp. 297–307.

[24] Erhard Haus, Michael H. Smolensky (1999), "Biologic rhythms in the immune system," *Chronobiology International*, vol. 16, pp. 581–622; Francis Lévi, Franz Halberg, Goro Chihara, J. Byram (1982), "Chronoimmunomodulation: Circadian, circaseptan and circannual aspects of immunopotentiation or suppression

with lentinan," in Ryō Takahashi, Franz Halberg, and Charles A. Walker, eds., *Toward Chronopharmacology*, Oxford: Pergamon Press, pp. 289–311.

[25] Salvador Sánchez de la Peña, Patricia Wood, Erna Halberg, et al. (1984), "Circadian and circaseptan aspects of malarial infection and cyclosporine treatment in mice," *Annual Review of Chronopharmacology*, vol. 1, pp. 411–414.

[26] Francis Lévi, Franz Halberg (1982), "Circaseptan: About 7 day rhythmsbioperiodicity –spontaneous and reactive –and the search for pacemakers," *La Ricerca in Clinica e in Laboratorio*, vol. 12, pp. 323–370; Francis Lévi, Franz Halberg, Goro Chihara, J. Byram (1982), "Chronoimmunomodulation: Circadian, circaseptan and circannual aspects of immunopotentiation or suppression with lentinan," in *Toward Chronopharmacology*, pp. 289–311; Ratte et al., 1977.

[27] K. Kawahara, Francis Lévi, Franz Halberg, et al. (1980), "Circaseptan bioperiodicity in rejection of heart and pancreas allografts in the rat," *Chronobiologia*, vol. 7, p. 13; K. Kawahara, Francis Lévi, Franz Halberg, et al. (1982), "Circaseptan bioperiodicity in rat allograft rejection," in *Toward Chronopharmacology, Proceedings 8th International Union of Basic and Clinical Pharmacology Congress and Satellite Symposium*, Nagasaki, 1981, July 27–28; Oxford: Pergamon Press, pp. 273–280; Jean Ratte, Franz Halberg, J. F. W. Kühl, J. Najarian (1977), "Circadian and circaseptan variations in rat kidney allograft rejection," in John P. McGovern, Alain E. Reinberg, and Michael H. Smolensky, eds., *Chronobiology in Allergy and Immunology*, Springfield, Ill: Charles C. Thomas, pp. 250–257.

[28] Eugene A. Cornelius, Edmund J. Yunis, Carlos Martinez (1967), "Parabiosis intoxication: Clinical hematologic, and

serologic features (abstract)," *Transplantation*, vol. 5, p. 112.

[29] Franz Halberg (1995), "The week in phylogeny and ontogeny: Opportunities for oncology," *In Vivo*, vol. 9, pp. 269–278; Francis Lévi, Franz Halberg (1982), "Circaseptan: About 7 day rhythms bioperiodicity –spontaneous and reactive –and the search for pacemakers," *La Ricerca in Clinica e in Laboratorio*, vol. 12, pp. 323–370; Francis Lévi, Franz Halberg, Goro Chihara, J. Byram (1982), "Chronoimmunomodulation: Circadian, circaseptan and circannual aspects of immunopotentiation or suppression with lentinan," in *Toward Chronopharmacology*, pp. 289–311; T. Liu, Marco Cavallini, Franz Halberg, et al. (1986), "More on the need for circadian, circaseptan and circannual optimization of cyclosporine therapy," *Experientia*, vol. 42, pp. 20–22.

[30] Charles DeLisi, Jacques R. J. Hiernaux, Franz Halberg (1983), "Circaseptan component of mammalian antibody production in response to immunization," *Chronobiologia*, vol. 10, p. 119.

[31] Eliane Bourreau, Paul Robel, Etienne-Emile Baulieu, et al. (1987), "Circaseptan (about 7-day) pregnenolone rhythm in brain and plasma of adrenalectomized and orchidectomized rats," *Cancer Detection and Prevention Journal*, vol. 11, p. 97.

[32] Keiko Uezono, Linda L. Sackett-Lundeen, Terukazu Kawasaki, Teruo Omae, Erhard Haus (1987), "Circaseptan rhythm in sodium and potassium excretion in salt-sensitive and salt-resistant Dahl rats," *Progress in clinical and biological research*, vol. 227A, pp. 297–307.

[33] John F. Araújo, A. S. F. Righini, J. J. Fleury, M. C. Caldas, J. B. Costa-Neto, N. Marques (1996), "Seasonal

rhythm of semen characteristics of a Brazilian Breed (Mangalarga) stallion," *Chronobiology International*, vol. 13, pp. 477–485; Nelson Marques, John Araújo, A. S. F. Righini, M. C. S. Caldas (1996), "Circaspetan rhythms of semen characteristics of a Brazilian breed (Mangalarga) stallion," *Biological Rhythm Research*, vol. 27, pp. 343–350.

[34] Giuseppe Piccione, Giovanni Caola, Robert Refinetti (2004), "Feeble weekly rhythmicity in hematological, cardiovascular, and thermal parameters in the horse," *Chronobiology International*, vol. 21, pp. 571–589.

[35] Ludwig Pöllmann (1984), "Wound healing-a Study on circaseptan reactive periodicity," *Chronobiology International*, 1:2, pp. 151–157, https://1ref.us/1p8 (accessed June 14, 2021).

[36] Germaine Cornélissen, D. Watson, Gen Mitsutake, Bohumil Fišer (2005), "Mapping of circaseptan and circadian changes in mood," *Scripta Medica* (Brno), vol. 78, pp. 89–98.

[37] Kuniaki Otsuka, Germaine Cornélissen, Franz Halberg (1994), "Broad scope of a newly developed actometer in chronobiology, particularly chronocardiology," *Chronobiologia*, vol. 21, pp. 251–264.

[38] Karl Hecht, Germaine Cornélissen, Ingo Fietze, et al. (2002), "Circaseptan aspects of self-assessed sleep protocols covering 70 nights on 33 clinically healthy persons," *Perceptual and Motor Skills*, vol. 95, pp. 258–266; Sarah-Jane Paine, Philippa H. Gander (2016), "Differences in circadian phase and weekday/weekend sleep patterns in a sample of middle-aged morning types and evening types," *Chronobiology International*, vol. 33, pp. 1009–1017.

[39] This cycle was recognized, in one study, for patients with scarlet fever. See Gunther Hildebrandt (1977),

"Hygiogenese. Grundlinien einer ther-apeutischen-physiologie," *Therapiewoche*, vol. 27, pp. 1911–1925. See also Franz Halberg, Christian Hamburger (1964), "17-ketosteroid and volume of human urines. Weekly and other changes with low frequency," *Minnesota Medicine*, vol. 47, pp. 916–925.

[40] Franz Halberg, Max Engeli, Christian Hamburger, Dewayne Hillmann (1965), "Spectral resolution of low-frequency small amplitude rhythms in excreted 17-ketosteroids: Probable androgen-induced circaseptan desynchronization," *Acta Endocrinology* (Kbh), vol. 103, pp. 5–54.

[41] Mikhail Blank, Germaine Cornélissen, Franz Halberg (1995), "Circasemiseptan (about-half-weekly) and/or circaseptan (about-weekly) pattern in human mitotic activity?" *In Vivo*, vol. 9, pp. 391–394. Franz Halberg (1995), "The week in phylogeny and ontogeny: Opportunities for oncology," *In Vivo*, vol. 9, pp. 269–278.

[42] Philippa J. Karoly, ME, Daniel M. Goldenholz, MD, Dean R. Freestone, PhD, Robert E. Moss, BS, David B. Grayden, PhD, William H. Theodore, MD, et al., "Circadian and circaseptan rhythms in human epilepsy: a retrospective cohort study," *The Lancet*, Sept. 12, 2018.

[43] Ruopeng An (2016), "Weekend-weekday differences in diet among U.S. adults, 2003–2012," *The Annals of Epidemiology*, vol. 26, pp. 57–65.

[44] Jimi Huh, Mariya Shiyko, Stefan Keller, et al. (2015), "The time-varying association between perceived stress and hunger within and between days," *Appetite*, vol. 89, pp. 145–151.

[45] Erhard Haus (2007), "Chronobiology of hemostasis and inferences for the chronotherapy of coagulation

disorders and thrombosis prevention," *Advanced Drug Delivery Reviews*, vol. 59, pp. 966–984; Erhard Haus, Michael H. Smolensky (1999), "Biologic rhythms in the immune system," *Chronobiology International*, vol. 16, pp. 581–622; Eugene L. Kanabrocki, Robert B. Sothern, W. Fraser Bremner, et al. (1995), "Weekly and yearly rhythms in plasma fibrinogen in hospitalized male military veterans," *American Journal Cardiology*, vol. 76, pp. 628–631; Francis Lévi, Franz Halberg (1982), "Circaseptan: About 7 day rhythms bioperiodicity –spontaneous and reactive –and the search for pacemakers," *La Ricerca in Clinica e in Laboratorio*, vol. 12, pp. 323–370.

[46] Ludwig Pöllmann (1984), "Wound healing –A study on circaseptan reactive periodicity," *Chronobiology International*, vol. 1, pp. 151–157.

[47] Gunther Hildebrandt (1984), "The time structure of adaptation," in Erhard Haus and Hugh F. Kabat, eds., *Chronobiology 1982–1983*, Basel: Karger, pp. 263–267.

[48] Hildebrandt (1984); C. Sasse (1981), "Über die Zeitstruktur des Adaptations-ver-laufes bei einem 4-wöchigen Ausdauerlei-stungstraining," Marburg/Lahn: Med Inaug Diss.

[49] A. De Vecchi, Franca Carandente, D. S. Fryd, et al. (1979), "Circaseptan (about 7-day) rhythm in human kidney allograft rejection in different geographic locations," in Alain E. Reinberg and Franz Halberg, eds., *Chronopharmacology*, Oxford: Pergamon Press, pp. 193–202; A. De Vecchi, Franz Halberg, Robert B. Sothern, et al. (1981), "Circaseptan rhythmic aspects of rejection in treated patients with kidney transplant," in Charles A. Walker, Charles M. Winget, and Karam F. A. Soliman, eds., *Chronopharmacology and Chronotherapeutics*, Tallahassee,

Florida: Florida A & M University Foundation, pp. 339–353; M. S. Knapp, R. Pownall (1980), "Biological rhythm in cell-medicated immunity: Findings from rats and men and their potential clinical relevance," in Michael H. Smolensky, Alain E. Reinberg, and John P. McGovern, eds., *Recent Advances in the Chronobiology of Allergy and Immunology*, Oxford: Pergamon Press, pp. 323–331.

[50] K. Hübner (1969), "Die periodik der DNS-synthese nach unspe-zifischen reizen," *Archives of Physical Therapy* (Leipz), vol. 21, pp. 251–260.

[51] Germaine Cornélissen, Franz Halberg, H. W. Wendt, et al. (1996), "Resonance of about-weekly human heart rate rhythm with solar activity change," *Biologia* (Bratisl), vol. 51, pp. 749–756; Kuniaki Otsuka, Gaku Yamanaka, Makoto Shinagawa, et al. (2004), "Chronomic community screening reveals about 31% depression, elevated blood pressure and infradian vascular rhythm alteration," *Biomedicine & Pharmacotherapy*, vol. 58, pp. S48–55; Makoto Shinagawa, Kuniaki Otsuka, Shogo Murakami, et al. (2002), "Seven-day (24-h) ambulatory blood pressure monitoring, self-reported depression and quality of life scores," *Blood Pressure Monitoring*, vol. 7, pp. 69–76.

[52] R. Peyró, J. R. Fernández, R. C. Hermida (1999a), "Prominent circaseptan pattern of invasive radial and pulmonary blood pressures in critical care patients," *Chronobiology International*, vol. 16, p. 84; R. Peyró, R. C. Hermida, J. R. Fernández (1999b), "Circadian variability of invasive blood pressure in patients interned in a critical care unit," *Chronobiology International*, vol. 16, p. 85.

[53] Mary S. Lee, John S. Lee, Jong Y. Lee, Germaine Cornélissen, Kuniaki Otsukab, Franz Halberg (2003), "About 7-day (circaseptan) and circadian changes in cold

pressor test (CPT)," *Biomedicine & Pharmacotherapy*, vol. 57, pp. 39s–44s.

[54] E. Radha, Franz Halberg (1987), "Rhythms of isolated platelet glutathione, aging and the internal evolution of species," in John E. Pauly and Lawrence E. Scheving, eds., *Advances in Chronobiology*, New York: Alan R. Liss, pp. 173–180.

[55] Dobroslav Hájek, Beata Šimčíková, Jiří Vorlíček (1993), "Circaseptan rhythm restitution by means of timed high dose methylprednisolon—an improvement of cytostatic treatment response?" *Journal of Interdisciplinary Cycle Research*, vol. 24, pp. 342–344.

[56] Francis A. Levi, Franz Halberg, "Circaseptan (about 7-day) bioperiodicity—spontaneous and reactive—and the search for pacemakers," see *La Ricerca en Clinica e in Laboratorio*, Apr-Jun 1982. 17-ketosteroids (substances formed when male adrenal hormones are released) See Germaine Cornélissen, David E. Axelrod, Franz Halberg (2004), "About-weekly variations in nocturia," *Biomedicine & Pharmacotherapy*, vol. 58, pp. S140–144.

[57] Natalia Rakova, Kathrin Jüttner, Anke Dahlmann, Agnes Schröder, Peter Linz, Christoph Kopp, Manfred Rauh, Ulrike Goller, Luis Beck, Alexander Agureev, Galina Vassilieva, Liubov Lenkova, Bernd Johannes, Peter Wabel, Ulrich Moissl, Jörg Vienken, Rupert Gerzer, Kai-Uwe Eckardt, Jens Titze (2013), "Long-term space flight simulation reveals infradian rhythmicity inhuman Na+balance," *Cell Metabolism*, vol. 17, pp. 125–131; Jens Titze, Anke Dahlmann, Kathrin Lerchl, et al. (2014), "Spooky sodium balance," *Kidney International*, vol. 85, pp. 759–767.

[58] Jens Kirchner, S. Paule, Claudia Beckendorf, S. Achenbach (2015), "Circadian and circaseptan rhythms in implant-based thoracic impedance," *Physiological Measurement*, vol. 36, pp. 1615–1628.

[59] "Thoracic impedance," available at https://1ref.us/1p (accessed June 14, 2021).

[60] Franz Halberg, R. Günther, M. Herold, Erna Halberg (1981), "Circadian and circaseptan (about 7-day) synchronization of urinary cortisol by ACTH in arthritics," *Proceedings of the Society for Endocrinology*, p. 331 (abstract 994).

[61] "What is Cortisol? Here's How it Impacts Your Body When You're Stressed," available at https://1ref.us/1pa (accessed June 14, 2021).

[62] Christian Hamburger (1954), "Six years' daily 17-ketosteroids determination on one subject; seasonal variations and independence of volume of urine," *Acta Endocrinology*, vol. 17, pp. 116–127; Franz Halberg, Alain Reinberg (1967), "Rythmes circadiens et rythmes de basses fréquences en physiologie humaine," *Journal of Physiology* (Paris), vol. 59, pp. 165–169 ; Franz Halberg, Max Engeli, Christian Hamburger, Dewayne Hillmann (1965), "Spectral resolution of low-frequency small amplitude rhythms in excreted 17-ketosteroids: Probable androgen-induced circaseptan desynchronization," *Acta Endocrinology* (Kbh), vol. 103, pp. 5–54; Christian Hamburger (1954), "Six years' daily 17-ketosteroids determination on one subject; seasonal variations and independence of volume of urines," *Acta Endocrinologica*, vol. 17, pp. 116–127; Christian Hamburger, Robert B. Sothern, Franz Halberg (1985), "Circaseptans and semicircaseptan aspects of human male sexual activity," *Chronobiologia*, vol. 12, p. 250.

[63] Franz Halberg, Alain Reinberg (1967), "Rythmes circadiens etrythmes de basses fréquences en physiologie humaine," *Journal of Physiology* (Paris), vol. 59, pp. 165–169; Franz Halberg, Max Engeli, Christian Hamburger, Dewayne Hillmann (1965), "Spectral resolution of low-frequency small amplitude rhythms in excreted 17-ketosteroids: Probable androgen-induced circaseptan desynchronization," *Acta Endocrinology* (Kbh), vol. 103, pp. 5–54.

[64] Christian Hamburger, Robert B. Sothern, Franz Halberg (1985), "Circaseptans and semicircaseptan aspects of human male sexual activity," *Chronobiologia*, vol. 12, p. 250.

[65] Diana E. Ayala, Ramón C. Hermida (1995), "Multifrequency infradian variation in blood pressure during and after pregnancy," *Chronobiology International*, vol. 12, pp. 333–343.

[66] Fulvio Agrimonti, Roberto Frairia, Daniela Fornaro, et al. (1984), "Circadian and circaseptan rhythmicities in corticosteroid-binding globulin (CBG) binding activity of human milk," in *Chronobiology 1982–1983*, pp. 234–238.

[67] Germaine Cornélissen, Mark Engebretson, Dana Johnson, et al. (2001), "The week, inherited in neonatal human twins, found also in geomagnetic pulsations in isolated Antarctica," *Biomedicine & Pharmacotherapy*, vol. 55, pp. 32s–50s. Leopoldo García, Ramón C. Hermida, Diana E. Ayala, et al. (1994), "Endogenous circaseptan variation in neonatal blood pressure. Biological rhythms and medications," *Proceedings of the Sixth International Conference of Chronopharmacology and Chronotherapeutics*, 1994 Jul 5–9; Amelia Island, Florida (U.S.A.), Abstract IIIb-3; Leopoldo García,

Ramón C. Hermida, Diana E. Ayala, A. Vázquez (1995), "Reproducible endogenous circaseptan variation in neonatal blood pressure (Abstract)," *Biological Rhythm Research*, vol. 26, pp. 392–393; C. Hurley, Brunetto Tarquini, Paolo T. Scarpelli, et al. (1987), "Further steps toward a neonatal chronocardiology," in Gunther Hildebrandt, Rudolf Moog, and Friedhart Raschke, eds., *Chronobiology and Chronomedicine: Basic Research and Applications*, Frankfurt: Verlag Peter Lang, pp. 288–292; Jian-Yong Wu, Germaine Cornélissen, Brunetto Tarquini, et al. (1990), "Circaseptan and circannual modulation of circadian rhythms in neonatal blood pressure and heart rate," *Progress in Clinical and Biological Research*, vol. 341A, pp. 643–652.

[68] Gérard Debry, R. Bleyer, Alain Reinberg (1975), "Circadian, circannual and other rhythms in spontaneous nutrient and caloric intake of healthy four-year olds," *Diabète & Métabolisme*. (Paris), vol. 1, pp. 91–99; Charles M. FitzGerald (1998), "Do enamel microstructures have regular time dependency? Conclusions from the literature and a large-scale study," *Journal of Human Evolution*, vol. 35, pp. 371–386.

[69] Claire Beugnet-Lambert, Alain Lancry, Pierre Leconte (1988), *Chronopsychologie*, Lille: Presses Universitaires de Lille, 342 pp. Nicole Guérin, Suzanne Boulenguier, Alain E. Reinberg, Geneviéve Di Costanzo, Philippe Guran, and Yvan Touitou (1993), "Weekly changes in psychophysiological variables of 8- to 10-year old school girls," *Chronobiology International*, vol. 10, pp. 471–479; Franz Halberg and Alain E. Reinberg (1967), "Rythmes circadiens etrythmes de basses fréquences en physiologie humaine," *Journal of Physiology* (Paris), vol. 59, pp. 165–169; Claire Leconte (2011), "Des rythmes de vie aux rythms

scolaires," Lille: Presses Universiaires du Spetentrion, 217 pp.; Pierre Leconte and Claire Leconte-Lambert, eds. (1990), *La chronopsychologie*, Paris: Presses Universitaires de France, Coll. "Que saisje?" No. 2549, 128 pp. Alain E. Reinberg (1997a), *Rythmes scolaires et rythmes biologiques de l'enfant*, Paris: Encyclopedia Universali, pp. 302–304; Alain E. Reinberg (1997b), *Les rythmes biologiques*, 7th ed. (1st ed., 1964), Paris: Presses Universitaires de France, "Que saisje?" 128 pp. Alain E. Reinberg (1998), *Le temps humain et les rythmes biologique*, Paris: Le Rocher, 250 pp. François Testu (1989), *Chronopsychologie et rythmes scolaires*, Paris: Masson, 120 pp. G. Vermeil (1995), *La fatigue à l'école*, Paris: Editions Sociales Françaises, 144 pp.

[70] Hobart A. Reimann, ed., *Periodic diseases*, Oxford: Blackwell Scientific Publ., 1963, 189 pp. Hobart A. Reimann (1971), "Haemocytic periodicity and periodic disorders: Periodic neutropenia, thrombocytopenia, lymphocyctosis, and anaemia," *Postgraduate Medical Journal*, vol. 47, pp. 504–510.

[71] Vladeta Ajdacic-Gross, Ulrich S. Tran, Matthias Bopp, G. Sonneck (2015). "Understanding weekly cycles in suicide: An analysis of Austrian and Swiss data over 40 years," *Epidemiology and Psychiatric Sciences*, vol. 24, pp. 315–321; Akerke Baibergenova, Lehana Thabane, Noori Akhtar-Danesh, Mitchell Levine, Amiram Gafni, Rahim Moineddin, and Indra Pulcins (2005), "Effect of gender, age, and severity of asthma attack on patterns of emergency department visits due to asthma by month and day of the week," *European Journal of Epidemiology*, vol. 20, pp. 947–956; Gillian A. Beauchamp, Mona L. Ho, Shan Yin (2014), "Variation in suicide occurrence by day and during major American holidays," *Journal of Emergency Medicine*, vol. 46, pp. 776–781; Judith C. Brillman, Tom Burr, David

Forslund, Edward Joyce, Rick Picard, and Edith Umland (2005), "Modeling emergency department visit patterns for infectious disease complaints: Results and application to disease surveillance," *BMC Medical Informatics and Decision Making*, vol. 5, p. 4; Pietro Cugini, Alfredo Romit, Loredana Di Palma, Mario Giacovazzo (1990), "Common migraine as a weekly and seasonal headache," *Chronobiology International*, vol. 7, pp. 467–469; Franz Halberg (1995), "The week in phylogeny and ontogeny: Opportunities for oncology," *In Vivo*, vol. 9, pp. 269–278; Li-Ting Kao, Ming-Chieh Tsai, Herng-Ching Lin, Femi Pai and Cha-Ze Lee (2010), "Weekly pattern of emergency room admissions for peptic ulcers: A population-based study," *World Journal of Gastroenterology*, vol. 21, pp. 3344–3350; Li-Ting Kao, Sudha Xirasagar, Kuo-Hsuan Chung, Herng-Ching Lin, Shih-Ping Liu, Shiu-Dong Chung (2014), "Weekly and holiday-related patterns of panic attacks in panic disorder: A population-based study," *PLoS One*, vol. 9, p. e100913; Roberto Manfredini, Benedetta Boari, Gabriele Anania, Giorgio Cavallesco (2015), "Seasonal and weekly patterns of hospital admissions for acute diverticulitis," *European Review for Medical and Pharmacological Sciences*, vol. 19, pp. 54–63; Cecilie Svanes, Robert B. Sothern, Halfdan Sørbye (1998), "Rhythmic patterns in incidence of peptic ulcer perforation over 5.5 decades in Norway," *Chronobiology International*, vol. 15, pp. 241–264; T. W. Walker, T. V. Macfarlane, G. W. McGarry (2007), "The epidemiology and chronobiology of epistaxis: An investigation of Scottish hospital admissions 1995–2004," *Clinical Otolaryngology*, vol. 32, pp. 361–365.

[72] H. R. Arntz, S. N. Willich, C. Schreiber, et al. (2000), "Diurnal, weekly and seasonal variation of sudden death. Population-based analysis of 24,061 consecutive cases," *European Heart Journal*, vol. 21, pp. 315–320; Benedetta

Boari, Elisa Mari, Massimo Gallerani, et al. (2011), "Temporal variation of heart failure hospitalization: Does it exist?" *Reviews in Cardiovascular Medicine*, vol. 12, pp. 211–218; K. Cantwell, A. Morgans, K. Smith, et al. (2015), "Temporal trends in cardiovascular demand in EMS: Weekday versus weekend differences," *Chronobiology International*, vol. 32, pp. 731–738; Germaine Cornélissen, T. K. Breus, C. Bingham, et al. (1993), "Beyond circadian chronorisk: Worldwide circaseptan-circasemi-septan patterns of myocardial infarctions, other vascular events and emergencies," *Chronobiologia*, vol. 20, pp. 87–115; R. Díaz-Sandoval, Salvador Sánchez de la Peña, A. Chávez-Negrete (2008), "Seven and 3.5-day rhythms in the incidence of my ocardiopathies in Mexico," *Archives of Medical Research*, vol. 39, pp. 134–813; Roberto Manfredini, Rodolfo Citro, Mario Previtali, Olga Vriz, Quirino Ciampi, Marco Pascotto, Ercole Tagliamonte, Gennaro Provenza, Fabio Manfredini, Eduardo Bossone, Takotsubo Italian Network investigators (2010a), "Monday preference in onset of takotsubo cardiomyopathy," *American Journal of Emergency Medicine*, vol. 28, pp. 715–719; Roberto Manfredini, Fabio Manfredini, Benedetta Boari, et al. (2010b), "Temporal patterns of hospital admissions for transient ischemic attack: A retrospective population-based study in the Emilia-Romagna region of Italy," Clinical and Applied Thrombosis/Hemostasis, vol. 16, pp. 153–160; Roberto Manfredini, Fabio Fabbian, Marco Pala, et al. (2011), "Seasonal and weekly patterns of occurrence of acute cardiovascular dis-eases: Does a gender difference exist?" *Journal of Women's Health* (Larchmt.), vol. 20, pp. 1663–1668; G. Y. Nicolau, Erhard Haus, M. Popescu, et al. (1991), "Circadian, weekly, and seasonal variations in cardiac mortality, blood pressure, and catecholamine excretion," *Chronobiology International*, vol. 8, pp. 149–

159; José Vitale, Roberto Manfredini, Massimo Gallerani, Nicola Mumoli, Kim A. Eagle, Walter Ageno, and Francesco Dentali (2015a), "Chronobiology of acute aortic rupture or dissection: Asystematic review and a meta-analysis of the literature," *Chronobiology International*, vol. 32, pp. 385–394; Daniel R. Witte, Diederick E. Grobbee, Michiel L. Bots, Arno W. Hoes (2005), "A meta-analysis of excess cardiac mortality on Monday," *European Journal of Epidemiology*, vol. 20, pp. 401–406.

[73] Erhard Haus, "Chronobiology in the endocrine system," *Advanced Drug Delivery Reviews*, vol. 59 (2007), pp. 985–1014.

[74] J. Guan, C. You, Y. Liu, et al. (2011), "Characteristics of infradian and circadian rhythms in the persistent vegetative state," *Journal of International Medical Research*, vol. 39, pp. 2281–2287.

[75] Franz Halberg, Alain E. Reinberg (1967), "Rythmes circadiens et rythmes de basses fréquences en physiologie humaine," *Journal of Physiology* (Paris), vol. 59, pp. 165–169; Franz Halberg, Alain E. Reinberg, Erhard Haus, et al. (1970), "Human biological rhythms during and after several months of isolation under-ground in natural caves," *Bulletin of the National Speleological Society*, vol. 32, pp. 89–115.

[76] https://1ref.us/1pb (accessed June 14, 2021).

[77] Erhard Haus, *Chronobiology in the Endocrine System*, *Advanced Drug Delivery Reviews*, vol. 59 (2007), pp. 985–1014.

[78] Francis Lévi, Franz Halberg (1982), "Circaseptan: About 7 day rhythms bioperiodicity –spontaneous and reactive –and the search for pacemakers," *La Ricerca

in Clinica e in Laboratorio, vol. 12, pp. 323–370; E. A. Lucas, Franz Halberg, K. D. Straub, et al. (1985), "About 7-day (circaseptan) free-running rhythms in urinary norepinephrine and systolic and diastolic blood pressure during human social isolation studies (Abstract)," *Journal of Sleep Research*, vol. 14, p. 305; M. Montalbini, A. Galvagno, S. Follini, et al. (1989), "Cardiovascular about-24-hour (circadian) and about-7-day (circaseptan) rhythms in human social isolation (Abstract)," Health of Inner Cities and Urban Areas, International Conference, Cardiff, Wales, 1989, September 4–7, *The Institute of Statisticians/SIRMCE*, p. 101; Salvador Sánchez de la Peña, Franz Halberg, A. Galvagno, et al. (1989), "Circadian and circaseptan (about-7-day) free-running physiologic rhythms of a woman in social isolation," *Proceedings of the 2nd Annual IEEE Symposium on Computer-Based Medical Systems*, Minneapolis, 1989 Jun 26–27, Washington DC: Computer Society Press, pp. 273–278.

[79] ("Possible natural circaseptan rhythm in the beach beetle *Chaerodes trachyscelides* White")

[80] Gunther Hildebrandt (1977), "Hygiogenese. Grundlinien einer ther-apeutischen-physiologie," *Therapiewoche* vol. 27, pp. 1911–1925; Gunther Hildebrandt, G. Geyer, W. Brünning (1982), "Circaseptan adaptive periodicity and weekly rhythms," in Gunther Hildebrandt and Herbert Hensel, eds., *Biological adaptation*, Stuttgard: Georg Thiem Verlag, pp. 113–116; Gunther Hildebrandt (1984), "The time structure of adaptation," in *Chronobiology 1982–1983*, pp. 263–267; Gunther Hildebrandt (1993), "Reactive modifications of the autonomous time structure of biological functions in man," *Annali dell'Istituto superiore di sanita*, vol. 29, pp. 545–557; Ludwig Pöllmann (1984), "Wound Healing –A

Study on Circaseptan Reactive Periodicity," *Chronobiology International*, vol. 1, pp. 151–157.

[81] Francis Lévi, Franz Halberg, Goro Chihara, J. Byram (1982), "Chronoimmunomodulation: Circadian, circaseptan and circannual aspects of immunopotentiation or suppression with lentinan," in *Toward Chronopharmacology*, pp. 289–311; Hanz Kaiser, G. Cornelissen, Franz Halberg (1990), "Palaeochronobiology circadian rhythms, gauges of adaptive Darwinian evolution: about 7-day (circaseptan) rhythms, gauges of integrative internal evolution," in Dora K. Hayes, John E. Pauly, and Russel J. Reiter, eds., *Chronobiology: Its Role in Clinical Medicine*, New York: Wiley-Liss Inc., pp. 755–762.

[82] Gunther Hildebrandt (1984), "The time structure of adaptation," in *Chronobiology 1982–1983*, pp. 263–267.

[83] Olivier Reinberg, Alain Reinberg, Mohamed Mechkouri (2005), "24-hour, weekly, and annual patterns in traumatic and non-traumatic surgical pediatric emergencies," *Chronobiology International*, vol. 22, pp. 353–381.

[84] John W. Ayers, B. M. Althouse, Morgan Johnson, et al. (2014a), "What's the healthiest day? Circaseptan (weekly) rhythms in healthy considerations," *American Journal of Preventive Medicine*, vol. 47, pp. 73–76; Elia Gabarron, Annie Y. S. Lau, Rolf Wynn (2015), "Is there a weekly pattern for health searches on Wikipedia and is the pattern unique to health topics?" *Journal of Medical Internet Research*, vol. 17, p. e286.

[85] Elia Gabarron, Annie Y. S. Lau, Rolf Wynn (2015), "Is there a weekly pattern for health searches on Wikipedia and is the pattern unique to health topics?" *Journal of Medical Internet Research*, vol. 17, p. e286.

[86] John W. Ayers, B. M. Althouse, Morgan Johnson, et al. (2014a), "What's the healthiest day? Circaseptan (weekly) rhythms in healthy considerations," *American Journal of Preventive Medicine*, vol. 47, pp. 73–76.

[87] John W. Ayers, B. M. Althouse, Morgan Johnson, Joanna E. Cohen (2014b), "Circaseptan (weekly) rhythms in smoking cessation considerations," *JAMA Internal Medicine*, vol. 174, pp. 146–148.

[88] Elia Gabarron, Annie Y. S. Lau, Rolf Wynn (2015), "Is there a weekly pattern for health searches on Wikipedia and is the pattern unique to health topics?" *Journal of Medical Internet Research*, vol. 17, p. e286.

[89] John W. Ayers, Benjamin M. Althouse, Morgan Johnson, Mark Dredze, and Joanna E. Cohen. (2014a), "What's the Healthiest Day? Circaseptan (Weekly) Rhythms in Healthy Considerations," *American Journal of Preventive Medicine*, vol. 47, pp. 73–76; John W. Ayers, B. M. Althouse, Morgan Johnson, Joanna E. Cohen (2014b), "Circaseptan (weekly) rhythms in smoking cessation considerations," *JAMA Internal Medicine*, vol. 174, pp. 146–148.

[90] He makes this point in discussing the five-day week of the Soviet Union. "Soviet workers may have rested more often than their Western counterparts (once every five, rather than seven, days), yet they certainly did not rest together, as one society, since 80 percent of the entire Soviet working population would be at work on any given day. ... Rather than merely alter the length of the week from a seven-day cycle to a five-day one, they essentially tried to destroy the idea of a common societal weekly cycle by abolishing the traditional Ju-deo-Christian institution of a single, uniform weekly day of rest that is commonly

shared by the entire society" (Eviatar Zerubavel, *The Seven Day Circle: The History and Meaning of the Week*, p. 37).

[91] Germaine Cornélissen, D. Watson, Gen Mitsutake, Bohumil Fišer (2005), "Mapping of circaseptan and circadian changes in mood," Scripta Medica (Brno), vol. 78, pp. 89–98

[92] Georg. B. et al. (2017) Melanopsin-expressing retinal ganglion cells are resistant, but not always. Mitochondrion (2017). 2006–2008.

[93] Cornelissen G et al (2002) Geomagnetics and Society interact in weekly and broader multiseptans underlying health and environmental integrity. Biomed Pharmacother 56 (2002) 319s-326s.

[94] The major papers employed in this booklet, which compiled other sources, are: Alain Reinberg, Laurence Dejardin, Michael H. Smolensky, and Yvan Touitou, "Seven-day human biological rhythms: An expedition in search of their origin, synchronization, functional advantage, adaptive value and clinical relevance," available at https://1ref.us/1pc (accessed June 14, 2021), Germaine Cornélissen, A. Portela, Franz Halberg, and V. Bolliet, "Toward a chronome of superfused pike pineals: About-weekly (circaseptan) modulation of circadian melatonin release," available at https://1ref.us/1pd (accessed June 14, 2021); V. Benno Meyer-Rochow and Philip J. Brown, "Possible natural circaseptan rhythm in the beach beetle *Chaerodes trachyscelides* White," https://1ref.us/1pe (accessed June 14, 2021).

TEACH Services, Inc.
P U B L I S H I N G

We invite you to view the complete
selection of titles we publish at:
www.TEACHServices.com

We encourage you to write us
with your thoughts about this,
or any other book we publish at:
info@TEACHServices.com

TEACH Services' titles may be purchased in
bulk quantities for educational, fund-raising,
business, or promotional use.
bulksales@TEACHServices.com

Finally, if you are interested in seeing
your own book in print, please contact us at:
publishing@TEACHServices.com

We are happy to review your manuscript at no charge.

www.ingramcontent.com/pod-product-compliance
Lightning Source LLC
Chambersburg PA
CBHW042133160426
43199CB00021B/2901